For Liam – may your contagious smile and beautiful mind continue to brighten this world.

I0161741

Why I'm Different
Understanding Autism

Don Eminizer
Christine Forget-Eminizer

Why I'm Different
Understanding Autism

Don Eminizer
Christine Forget-Eminizer

A 🍎 B 🐤 C 🚗 D 🦕 E 🐘

Hi! My name is Liam.
I'm in kindergarten.

I'm in a special classroom because I have special needs.

I look like any other kid... ...but I have autism. (aw-tis-uhm)

Autism is a condition that affects the way I act, Learn, and interact with other people.

Sometimes, people think I'm not smart or don't have feelings because of the way I behave.

Sometimes when I'm really excited I flap my hands and make loud noises.

I do this because I have a hard time controlling my emotions.

Some kids make fun of me because I'm still wearing diapers.

Learning to go potty is very difficult for me and I need encouragement. It's not nice to make fun of people!

...but there are still plenty of things we can do together!

Ask my parents or teachers for ideas of fun games for us to play!

Do you know other kids with special needs?

EPILEPSY

ADHD

HEARING impairment

ADD

APRAXIA

DOWN SYNDROME

BLINDNESS

CEREBRAL PALSY

DYSLEXIA

Tell your friends and help them understand how to interact with us!

www.Liamsbooks.com
Liamsbooks@99burning.com

www.ingramcontent.com/pod-product-compliance
Lightning Source LLC
Chambersburg PA
CBHW041806040426
42448CB00001B/55